Police Officers are involved in 400 killings every year

Over 18% are African Americans who are under the age of 21

Three teenaged African American boys walk down the streets of North Carolina after celebrating a night of each of them turning eighteen. Two Caucasian police officers in a squad car drive down the street watching them from up ahead as they pull up closer to the three teenage boys. The two police officers hear on the radio dispatch of a description of an African American suspect wanted for a convenient store robbery wearing a black hoody and a snap back hat. The two police officers look at the three teenage boys and see that all three of them are wearing snap back hats. The officer in the driver's seat steps on the gas speeding up to the three of them as the other officer switched the siren on to flash the lights. The squad car pulls up next to the side walk where the three teenage boys are walking. The three boys stop walking and stand together in confusion. The two police officers step out of the squad car and both say "Let's see some I.D.". The boy standing on the left raises his hand. "We don't have any". The two police officers both pull out a pen and a note pad. All of the boys look at the two police officer's badges reading the names and numbers on it. One officer's badge says Peter Stevens. The other police officer's badge says David O'neil. Officer Stevens goes up to the boy standing on the right. "What is your name"? "Darren Richards is my name". Officer Stevens looks at the other two boys. "What are your names"? "My name is Mike Williams". "My name is John Lawrence". Officer O'neil writes down all their names on his notepad. Officer Stevens stares at all three of them. "Where were you all coming from"? Mike sighs and nods his head. "We were just coming from John's cousin's house after we were all celebrating our birthday party". "Are you guys in high school or something"? All three of them nod their heads yes. "Well then do any of you have a school I.D."? All three of them nod their heads no. "Me and my partner received a call about a robbery in the area". Mike steps forward. "Like I said we were all just heading home from our birthday party". Officer Stevens glares at Mike. "I see that you're carrying a back pack, do you mind if I take a look at it"? "What do you want to look at it for"? "Because I want to make sure that I can trust you". Officer O'neil takes Darren and John over to the squad car and frisks them with their hands on the hood. Officer Stevens kneels down and zips open Mike's back pack taking out a pair of sneakers, a lighter, headphones, and a school textbook of biology. "Is there anything else in here you want to tell me about"? "No, I don't have anything else in there". Officer Stevens kneels back up and zips the back pack closed and hands it back to Mike. "Look officer I don't mean no disrespect but if I'm not home soon my mom is going to get worried and kill me when I get home". As long as you're telling me the truth then you'll make it home soon". "I'm sorry but I just don't know what we did" "Like I told you before there has been a robbery in the area but now I'm starting to believe you but what I need now is my partner to make sure you're friends check out and then you'll be good to go". "Just sit tight and I'm going to talk to my partner". Officer Stevens turns around and walks up to Officer O'neil, Darren, and John. Mike feels his cell phone vibrating in his pocket. He reaches in to pull it out. Officer O'neil glances at him. He sees him reaching into his pocket. "Look out"! Officer O'neil quickly pulls out his fire arm from his holster and fires three shots at Mike hitting him three times in the abdomen and chest. Mike drops down flat to the side walk with his cell phone falling out of his hand. Out of reaction Darren and John both put their heads down on the hood of the squad car with their hands on their head. Officer Stevens pulls out his fire arm. He immediately handcuffs Darren and John as they lie down on the hood. Officer O'neil runs up to Mike's body aiming his fire arm at him. He looks over at the cell phone next to him and picks it up. He checks it and sees that it says one missed call from one of the contacts that is labeled as mom. Officer Stevens puts  Darren and John into the back seat of the squad car. He walks up to officer O'neil. "What happened"? Officer O'neil hands him the cell phone. "I thought this was a gun". They both bend down and check Mike's pulse from his neck and wrist. Darren and John both look at Mike's body from the inside of the squad car. They both scream out "Mike, Mike, Mike"! Residents of the neighborhood and bystanders watch from across the street. Officer Stevens dispatches an ambulance from his walkie talkie. A few minutes later an ambulance truck pulls up along with three other police squad cars. Two paramedics strap Mike onto a stretcher and wheel him into the ambulance truck. Darren and John are driven to the nearest police precinct. Officer Stevens and O'neil write out a report as the other police officers hold back angry neighbors and bystanders. As Mike is driven away in the ambulance truck the thoughts that run through his mind are vivid memories of diary quotes he would write in class while he would sit at his desk. The words that play back in his head is all filled with frustration. One of the paramedics applies pressures on his abdomen to stop the bleeding. The words that play back in his head is "Will there ever be justice for my people"? "I'm sick and tired of being judged"! "In this present day we still need more heroes, and why not have it start with me". "Maybe one day we'll truly be free from being enslaved, inferior, 2nd class, and in these days be free from incarceration". Officer Stevenson and O'neil drive back to their precinct hearing on the radio dispatch that the suspect in the robbery has been apprehended. By midnight Michael Martin Williams is declared dead at the intensive care unit at the hospital. The next day Officer O'neil sits in a conference room at the police department with the commissioner. Sitting next to him is Officer Stevens. "Like my partner Peter explained we both stopped three African American males because from what we heard they all fit the description of a robbery suspect that we got dispatched for". "After me and Peter stopped them we asked if they had I.D. and then they said they didn't have any or refused to and then that is when we searched them". The commissioner squints his eyes at Officer O'neil. "Were you the one who searched the other two young men"? "That's right and when Peter was done searching the other one that is when he pulled out a cell phone which at the time I thought was a fire arm and that's when I opened fire out of reaction". Officer Peter and David walk back to their desks at the department and sit across from each other. David looks at Peter fidgeting with his hands. "What do you think is going to happen Peter"? "You mean from what the commissioner was saying"? "Well you saw what happened and it really was an accident and another thing is I don't want to be looked at as the big bad wolf because I was just out there doing my duty". "It's too bad we weren't the ones who brought in the right suspect from the robbery because if anything it might of took some heat off of us so that people don't think weren't just a bunch of trigger happy cowboys". "I know it really would've looked better if we were the ones who brought in the guy who committed the actual robbery but the fact is for awhile we're going to have to hear what people think of us out there and maybe even in here". "You know peter, I never came out and said this before but you really can't blame us for questioning those boys". "What do you mean"? "I'm just saying the way those type of people act and even talk should be obvious enough why people can see them as threatening". "You know that I'm not a racist but when you look and act a certain way you should expect to get treated a certain way". "I was thinking the same thing with all that gangster rap but when I talked to that kid Michael he seemed like he wasn't that bad". "Either way they should all know better and I hope you keep your word when you said you would take some responsibility for what happened because you searched his back pack but you didn't search him". "David I don't think anything else is going to happen from here on but I can't help thinking about what his parents said are what they might do". "He probably only has one parent because honestly he most likely doesn't even have a father". Later on that day David sits in his living room watching the news broadcasting the scene of where the shooting occurred and footage of African Americans marching and protesting. He watches on as he drinks down three bottles of alcohol one by one.

Two weeks before the shooting Mike walks home from school and goes into his bedroom. Next to his bed is a desk with a lap top and journal on it. He opens the journal and begins to write a new entry. In the paragraph he writes "I shut out all words like thug, ghetto, thief, and any words that can be used to judge and stereotype my culture". "May I or any of my brothers and sisters not be just only recognized for rhyming over a beat and a hook or dunking a ball in a hoop". "Although I may be thankful for any progress or adjustment that's been made over the years please don't let me be blinded by any one or anything". "I shall also never be haunted by words like darkness, ugliness, or color because the only color I see out of any body is red from the blood that we all bleed as humans". "When it is my time to make a life of my own the words that I want to hear that is chosen for me is words like doctor, lawyer, or anything that benefits my future so that I can benefit others". John walks up to the front door of the house and knocks on the door. Mike closes the journal and walks to the front door and opens it. "Hey John, where were you today"? "I had to finish my homework and you know how Mr. Wilson is when we didn't finish our work". "Yeah you're right". "Is anybody else here"? "No, my mom went to her church service". "So can I come in"? "Let's go to my room". They both go into Mike's bedroom. John sits on the chair by the desk. Mike sits on the bed. John grabs Mike's journal. "What do you write in this"? "Put that down man its private"! John puts the journal back on the desk. "Just wait I'll read it some time". "I'll start hiding it then". "Any way I came to see what you wanted to do for your birthday party since its on the same month of me and Darren's birthday". "I don't know yet, what were you thinking"? "When I talked to Darren he said he was planning on going over his cousin's house but then he said his cousin doesn't mind if we come with him". "I guess we can because I don't have anything else planned". "I can't believe after a few more months we'll finally be done with high school". "I can't wait till I don't have any more homework or exams to worry about". "What are your plans after we graduate Mike"? "I'm planning on going to college". "I'm not surprised, you're always writing or doing some kind of extra work". "I just want to try it out for a couple of years and see what else I can do". "All I know is I'm looking for a job so I can finally have enough to buy my own car". "Have you ever thought about going to college John"? "I don't know but for right know I'm tired of school". "Do you ever think about what you're going to do within the next five or ten years"? "I really don't, all I know is I need a break from school and I need to make some of that quick money". "I was thinking that if you wanted to join what I plan to do after I graduate college". "Which is"? "I want to start my own business with events like fund raisers and charities". "How did you get that idea"? "My mom always says with the way I help her out it can be used for more people". "I could see you doing something like that but with what kind of people"? "You know I always admired the work of Dr. Martin Luther King and Nelson Mandela so I figure maybe those are the type of foot steps I should follow in". "I thought you wanted to become more of a professional writer". "I do but I've been thinking maybe I should try more than just writing what's on my mind in a journal and start doing". "If I join what would we have to do to help people"? "As a start I want to help children in low income neighborhoods so that they don't follow down the path they already get judged for". "Its bad enough there is young men like us out there killing each other but then when there is no other solution they get locked up with little hope for a good future". "I know what you mean its hard every where you go". "I'd rather do something about it than sit back and watch it all happen over and over". "Mike, no matter what we have to look out for ourselves at all times and the only way we can do that is if we can all stick together". "Whatever you want to do after high school or college you know I always got your back". Three weeks later at the home of John's parents he and Darren are together in the living room with other young African American boys and girls. John stands up in front of all of them. "I can guarantee all of you that if Mike was white this would've never happened"! "Me, him, and Darren were just celebrating our birthday at my cousin's house and then we get stopped because to them all they see us is as thugs no matter where we go". "Me and Mike always talked about how frustrating it is for people like us especially in our age group to make try and make it in this country"! "I was always in denial on how hard it is for a black male to be success in America but of course Mike planned to go to college after we graduate and instead he's gone because society already had it's mind made up of who he was". "Then right before anything is cleared up me and Darren and get arrested with no questions asked, forcing us to call our parents in the middle of the night with them wondering why their sons are with the police in the first place". A camera man and a female news reporter knock on the door of Gloria William's house. She opens the door looking right at the camera. "Hello Mrs. Williams, I'm Julia Martinez from channel 4 news". "Do you have a moment to speak with us"? Gloria lets Julia and the camera man in. Gloria and Julia sit across from each other in the living room as the camera man films them. "We know this must be a difficult time for you right now but how are you feeling"? "No mother should ever have to bury their child but I know my son Michael is up there with god because all he wanted to do is help people and make sure we were always okay". Gloria wipes a tear from her eye. "How do you feel about the officer who claims to have mistakenly thought your son was carrying a fire arm"? "Only god can judge those who make mistakes". "If you don't mind me asking what does Michael's father think"? "Michael's father passed away when he was even years old from a head on crash shortly after me and him divorced". "I'm sorry to hear that, what do you plan to do going forward"? "My son planned on making a difference and I'm not going to let this change that". For the next two following months all around the united states along with North Carolina TV viewers from residences, bars, and store windows watch the broad casted court sessions of Officer David O'neil. After another week he was found not guilty of any charges the shooting of Michael Williams. After John sees the verdict on the news of Officer David O'neil being found not guilty he jumps up and storms into his room. He punches the wall with his fist. His father John Sr. runs in. "Come on son sit down". They both sit on the bed. "Being angry is not going to bring Michael back". "I know but I'm sick of this, all those cops get to harass us and nothing ever happens to them". "You can't always go by what you see or hear". "We should all get together and shut the city down". "If you do that then there will be more of you young men dead or in jail and for all for nothing". "Let me tell you something, no matter how something may appear things always even out the way they should in the end". During that same week there in each major city in America there is a march of African American protesters holding up pictures of Mike. In North Carolina the march is lead by Mike's mother Gloria. Next to her is John and Darren along with other class mates. Later on that night John purchases a 9mm pistol from an arms dealer on the street. He paces and down across the street from a coffee shop as he waits for police officers to show up. A moment later he sees one parked across the street that just pulled up. John walks across the street towards the police car with his head down. When he comes closer to the police car he taps on the window of the passenger side. The officer sitting on that side rolls down the window. John sees that the two police officers are Caucasian. He pulls out the 9mm and shoots both of them point blank in the head. Brain fragments splatter from the car to the outside in John's face. He runs away after firing one more shot in the officer's chest that is sitting in the passenger seat. He runs into an alley way and puts the 9mm into his mouth and pulls the trigger. John falls on a brick wall of the building in the alley way and slowly slides off it falling into a puddle. John stands across the street looking at the police squad car imagining it all in his head. He looks down a t his T-shirt seeing the picture of Mike on it. He walks away in a different direction and tosses the 9mm into a dumpster. As he continues to walk he flashes back to when him, Darren, and Mike blew out their candles on their birthday cake. He smiles and looks up at the sky with tears slowly dropping out of his eyes. Officer David once again sits in his living room drinking down a bottle of alcohol. He has flash backs of the shooting over and over. Glimpses of Mike's voice and face pop up in his head. He grabs a set of keys off the coffee table and walks outside. He drives away in a pick up truck. His vision is blurred as he continues to drive. He crosses over to the opposite side of the road. A car up ahead honks the horn. David crashes the pick up truck in a head collision to the other driver.


John Lawrence went on to College majoring in criminal justice after his high school graduation.


Officer Peter Stevenson resigned as a police officer.

Officer David O'neil is now serving a life sentence for a fatal hit and run while intoxicated.


Darren Richardson became a civil rights activist after graduation.


Gloria Williams opened up a child day care from fund raisers promoting anti-violence.


Dedicated To


Trayvon Martin

Oscar Grant

Michael Brown

Tamir Rice


Konichiwa


Rick Stone is an eighteen year old high school drop out in a youth street gang called "The PCF" which stands for pipes, chains, and fists in Bronx, New York. He spends most of his days wandering the streets all day with the four other members named Bobby The Monster, Danny Bullets, Tommy Bones, and Mikey Mouse. They isolate themselves from other gangs by race since their an all white gang. They consider their gang like an elite unit with the theme of older gangs by not using guns as often as the other gangs do but using them only when in real danger. They originally formed to protect themselves from Hispanic and African American gangs around the neighborhood. They run their own rackets of counterfeiting money, car jacking, and gambling. Along with their gun policy they also decide to ban any kind of drug dealing within their gang so that it doesn't draw too much attention to the other crimes that they commit. They base their philosophies on self defense and sometimes even being heroes to the poor. On this day they all sit on a park bench each smoking cigarettes. Each time a woman walks by they all shout whistle. Rick stands up and checks the time on his cell phone. "Don't you guys have anything better to do". Danny looks at him "Maybe we do but why"? "Sometimes I feel like I belong somewhere else but here". "Then let's take the train down to Amy's place, I'm sure her parents aren't still home". "I don't mean that I mean somewhere away from this whole city". "Just get first class tickets to Hawaii". Bobby and Mikey both laugh. "Come on guys I'm serious". "Don't tell me you're getting soft on us Ricky". "I should've known you guys wouldn't know any better". "Calm down man I'm just joking with you". Rick checks the time on his cell phone again. "Whatever I have to go check on my mother". Rick walks out off the park heading towards a bus stop. Danny sits back down. "What's up his ass"? Twenty minutes later Rick gets off the bus and walks upstairs to an apartment building as he hears dogs barking and neighbors yelling. He stops in front of one of the tenant doors on the third floor. He takes out a key and opens the door. "Mom, are you here"? She stands in the kitchen chopping up beef. "I'm in the kitchen". Rick walks into the living room looking at the mantle with pictures of war veterans that is in their family. He walks into the kitchen and sits on the table. He looks over and sees a stack of books on the other side of the table. "Where did you get these"? "I was down at the library earlier". Rick reaches over grabbing them. He looks through each one of them. At the bottom of the stack he sees a book that has teachings and research on samurai warriors from ancient Japan. That night Rick stays up reading through the whole book. He memorizes and takes in each lesson and stories from history. The next morning Danny, Bobby, and Mikey sit on the stoop of the apartment waiting for Rick. Right before Rick leaves the apartment he walks his mother in the living room. "Ma I'm going back out but I actually liked reading last night so right now I think I'm going to head to the library". "Okay see you later". Rick goes downstairs to meet up with Danny, Bobby, and Mikey. "Hey guys I want to stop some place before we head out". Bobby sighs. "Come on my cousin says he'll be around soon with the new car we were going to look at". "Yeah I know but I just want to go somewhere real quick or just all of you wait for me here and I'll be right back". Rick turns around and heads to the library. Danny, Bobby, and Mikey sit back down on the stoop rolling dice. A car pulls up in front of them. They look at it to see who it is. The driver rolls the window down. He waves a flag of Puerto Rico in his hand symbolizes a rival gang. Danny throws up his middle finger. The gang member in the passenger seat opens the glove compartment and pulls out a pistol. Danny and Bobby both stand up and pull out switch blade knives. The gang member gets out the car and points the pistol at them. Danny and Bobby both back up slowly. Mikey puts his hands up. The gang member gets back in the car and they both drive off. Danny watches the car drive away looking closely at the license's plate number. Rick sits down in the library talking to one of the librarians. "I read this one book last night and it really got be interested in reading more so I was wondering if you had anymore books on history". "I can help you with that". "Another thing is I've already been thinking different about things and I really do want to try different things for the better". "Well that's good as long as you do it while you're still young". "I was even thinking getting my G.E.D". "I wish more people around here would". "I would also like my friends to do the same but they couldn't listen even if they tried". "That's how must of them are". "I was thinking too that maybe after I do get my G.E.D I can move somewhere else". "You never know what's possible". Rick checks out of the library with a new book on crime history. When he walks towards Danny, Bobby, and Mikey he sees them arguing with each other. "Hey guys what's the problem"? Mikey grabs Rick by the arm. "These two guys came and pulled a gun out on us"! "Do any of you know them"? Rick looks at Danny. "I think I saw them a few weeks ago watching us". "I know what there car looks like and from what I remember where they stay is not that far from here". "Rick, we need to go after them tonight but first we need to go get that car". "What should we do if you said they had a gun"? "I know where we can get one but come on we need to go get that car". An hour later they sit in a new muscle car as Danny drives. Rick sits up front smoking a cigarette. "Now if we need to get a gun then fine but I would rather just whip him with a chain to send a message then just start shooting". "We need to show them so they don't come around again and I want one just in case we need it". Danny pulls up to a street corner. He walk up to a man wearing a trench coat. He gives the man a one hundred dollar bill. The man hands him a paper bag. Danny gets back into the car and drives off. He hands Rick the paper bag. Rick reaches into it and pulls out a gun which is a revolver. He opens the barrel seeing that it's loaded. Danny looks at him and smiles. "Alright let's get these assholes". They pull up in front of a chop shop garage. Rick pictures in his mind them being samurais riding into battle on their horses. All four of them quietly get out of the car. Rick hands Danny the revolver. Danny knocks on the front door of the shop. A teenage Hispanic girl answers the door. Danny grabs her my the mouth and pushes her back in holding the revolver up against her head. They all sneak in holding her as a hostage. They walk into the garage and three other gang members stand up glaring at them. The two they encountered with run up behind them. They wrestle with the gun in Danny's hand. The three other gang members fight with Rick, Bobby, and Mikey by throwing punches and grappling with each other. The teenage girl runs away screaming. The other gang member wrestles Danny to the ground trying to grab the gun. Danny reaches around his waist and whips out his switchblade knife. He slashes the gang member's right arm. The gang member falls down holding his arm as it bleeds. Danny gets up and pulls the trigger. The sound makes everyone else stop fighting. They all stop to look. They see the gang member down with a bloody bullet hole through his head. Another shot is fired from a different direction and it hits Danny in the chest. He falls to the floor next to the gang member. They all look over and see the teenage girl crying with a pistol in her hand. Rick runs up to Danny. Bobby and Mikey both grab him and they run back outside. The rest of the gang members and the girl run out the other way. Rick starts the car and drives off with Bobby and Mikey. By the time the police get there Danny and the gang member are found both dead. Two days later Bobby and Mikey both get caught and arrested as accomplices. Bobby turns in Rick for proving Rick's finger prints on the revolver. After Bobby gets let go Rick gets arrested and his sentenced along with Mikey. During his he entered good behavior programs and finally received his G.E.D. Three years later Rick gets released. When he walks out through the prison gates he says to himself "For a samurai warrior it' an honor to die in battle". After finding stable work Rick moved out off New York and traveled. Bobby was found dead in an alley way from a heroin over dose. After Mikey's release he was rearrested after being caught with counterfeit currency. Rick settled in Tokyo, Japan working in teaching philosophy.

The end


Locked Down

John Simmons is a Twenty eight year old death row inmate from Florida waiting for his sentence of lethal injection in a week. He is now under twenty three hour lock down for fighting two days with another inmate In the cafeteria. In the cell he's in now he sits at a small desk with a pen and a pile of lined paper. He takes one of the pieces of paper out of the pile and takes the cap off the pen. Before he begins to write he goes over the memories of his trial and what he's been charged with. The first memory he thinks of is when he was seventeen years old and he got sent to a juvenile boot camp for slashing a students face with switchblade knife at the high school he used to go to. Then during those days of his youth he thinks of times when he lived at home just with his father who would always drink alcohol excessively and physically abuse him. John never knew who his mother was only hearing her come up in conservations saying that she committed suicide. When he turned eighteen he chooses to runaway and drift on the streets. He packs his clothes into a book bag and sneaks to get his father's pistol from his wardrobe. Right before he walks out the door he sees his father passed out on the living room floor. He nods his head and walks out the door. When he wanders around in the streets he spends his days mugging people in alley ways at gun point. Then by the end of the day he uses the money to buy food and to rent a motel. Then after two months of doing the same pattern he gets arrested and gets sentenced to three years in prison. During his first time of incarceration since he is still a young man he was taken advantage of by the older inmates. During his first year of sentencing the trauma causes him to have mental and emotional break downs. This lead him to have to be cared for in the psychiatric unit. After serving a year and a half of the three year sentence he was released on parole. When he got out he had no money and no place to go. He returned to the streets but this time he wandered around looking for any kind of job that's hiring. Each time he fills out an application he gets turned down because of the armed robbery felony on his record. The frustrations of not being able to find work causes him to build up more and more anger. He sits on a park bench all day drinking a bottle of whiskey. Then over night he sleeps on the park bench. The next day he walks the streets looking around at different people he passes by. Then as he walks on he sees an open truck parked out back of a bakery shop. Behind the truck he sees a van parked aside with two men suspiciously looking around to see if the area is clear. John walks up to them. They both pull out revolvers and aim at him "Just go about your business Mr."! John scratches his head. "Do you guys need any help"? The two men look at each other in confusion. "Oh and in case if you wondering if I'm a cop". John lifts up his shirt and shows all of his prison tattoos. "I say again, do you guys need any help"? They both put away their revolvers. "Go to that truck over there and help us load those boxes into this van". "All three of them quickly run back and fourth loading the boxes into the van from the truck. A few minutes later they finish up and quickly drive off in the van. A chef from the bakery runs out and sees that the back of the truck is completely empty. After John and the two other men drive off they stop at a street corner in front of a warehouse. John helps them unload the boxes into the warehouse. When their done John gets paid two hundred dollars in cash. Before they leave he asks them "Do you have any other work like this because I could really use the money". From then on John worked with the group of men in merchandise robberies, loan sharking, and occasionally gambling. Since John had become a hardened inmate for the loan sharking they sent John to collect by using intimidation. Each time he would either do it by gun point or by a beating with his fists. With the money that John got he bought himself a car and an apartment. In John's cell he writes all of these memories down. Outside the cell door he hears the warden through the intercom say "Lights Out"! He stops writing and goes to bed. The next he continues to write. This he goes deeper into the past of the trial that got him on death row. By the end of the trial he was convicted with four counts of murder. When he thinks back to how it all started he thinks of when his rackets of robbery and loan sharking came to an end when all of his partners got arrested on other charges. This caused him to go bankrupt and he receives eviction notices to his apartment. From this all of his anger and frustration build up again. He goes out on a drinking binge spending each night in bars. His first murder victim was a bartender who he stabbed after the bar was closed for refusing to give him anymore drinks. The second murder victim was a strangled prostitute found in the trunk of a car at a pier. The third murder victim was a gambler he shot in the head who owed him money from betting on a football game. The fourth victim was a woman he clubbed to death with a pistol from an attempted purse snatch. As John writes this all down he crumbles up the paper ad throws it into the trash barrel. He writes on a new piece of paper referring himself as a man named John Dawson. As he writes on he fantasizes himself as a successful lawyer owning a house in a suburban neighborhood with a wife and a son a daughter. He pictures himself getting up every morning having breakfast with his wife and kids and then heading to the firm carrying his brief case. From then on he pictures all of his murder victims playing an opposite role as something positive in his life. He sees the bartender as a caterer at him and his wife's wedding. He sees the prostitute as his secretary at the firm. He sees the gambler as a family friend who comes over for cook outs. He also sees the woman with the purse a friend of his wife. He even sees the men he did robberies with as fellow lawyers he works with who go golfing and fishing with him. A week goes by and it's the day of John execution. When he is escorted out of his cell by the guards he visions each inmate he walks by as being their own desired fantasies. As John walks in and sees the chair he closes his eyes and pictures a day that would be his last and how he would want it to end. It's of him walking down the street handing out one hundred dollar bills to strangers and donating food to children. The last thing he pictures is his mother alive and his father growing old together watching him and his children in the backyard of his house. The guards sit him down and strap him to the chair. Right before the shot is injected into him he looks on smiling picturing his last day of everyone whose ever been in his life celebrating all of his happiness.

THE END


Insanity

Jimmy Thompson was a newly graduate from high school. To this day he still struggles with an obsession with a girl named Mary Miller. He has known her since middle school in eighth grade. The first they met was at a dance that the school was having. At that time Jimmy only kept close to a couple of people who were two other students named James and Zachary. On that day of the dance. Mary was looking for someone to dance with. She saw Jimmy sitting by himself isolated from everyone else. Out of kindness she walks up to him and says "Do you want to dance"? Out of excitement he stands up responding "Sure, let's go". They both join the rest of the students and dance together until it was time to go home. Before they both leave Mary gives Jimmy a hug. "Thanks, see you later". Jimmy pauses out of surprise. "Yeah see you later". Mary turns around to leave. Jimmy watches her walk away as starts to become more and more infatuated. At this time it's close to the end of the school year. On the last of graduation for the eighth graders Jimmy spots Mary walking outside with her friends. He comes up behind her. "Hey Mary am I going to see you in high school next year"? She turns her head as she keeps walking. "Yeah I'll be there". "Okay see you then". The summer of that year at a birthday party of his friend James in the backyard of his house  Jimmy sees Mary coming in with her own mutual friends. Right when Jimmy sees her his nerves get worked up. For the first hour of the party Jimmy sits aside nervously again isolated from everyone else watching on as they swim in the pool and socialize eating birthday cake. Another minute later he gets up and walks over towards Mary as she sits with friends beside the pool. He stands in front of her. She looks at him. "Oh hi Jimmy". "Hey Mary do you think we can talk in private for a second". Mary thinks for a moment. "Okay sure". She gets up and they walk over to the corner where he was just sitting. "What do you need to talk to me about"? "Oh not much I just think you're great and I haven't had this much fun in a long time and I actually do feel something for you". Jimmy's palms start to sweat. "That's real sweet Jimmy". "So how do you feel about that"? Mary looks away for a minute unsure on what to say. "What, are you seeing somebody"? She looks back at him. "Yes his name is Chris McDonough". Jimmy looks down out of discouragement. "I'm sorry but I do think you're a great guy and I only think of you as a friend". Mary turns to look at her friends. "Well I got to get back see you later". She walks away heading back over to sit beside the pool. Jimmy walks out of the backyard into the street. He sits on the sidewalk curb trying to hold himself back from crying. Later that day when he gets dropped off back home he walks in on both of his parents shouting and arguing. He goes straight to his bedroom and sits on his bed. He looks back on bad memories from child hood. Like him being bullied in school, domestic violence between relatives, Seeing Mary with someone else and not ever being close to either of his parents. All of these thoughts build up a rage inside Jimmy. Out of reaction he punches three wholes into his bedroom wall. Then he takes apart his dresser drawer and throws his clothes all around the bedroom. When he runs out of energy he sits back down on the bed slapping himself in the face. The next year as a freshmen in high school he still carried on the anger from last year. Sometimes he would see Mary and Chris walking together. Each time he would look away trying to pretend they're not there. For that whole year Jimmy struggled through emotions getting jealous each time he seen other couples walking around. Until the year ended Jimmy was too nervous and upset set to even talk to a girl or even Mary again even though this whole time his feelings for her never changed. He has it in his mind made up that next year she won't be with Chris anymore and be fate he'll ask her out again and then this time she'll say yes. When next year came around as sophomores one day Jimmy saw Mary in the cafeteria by herself but not with Chris. From the other day word got around that she and Chris had broke up. Jimmy walks up to her with nerves once again building up. He approaches her saying "Hey Mary how are you"? "I'm good hi Jimmy". As he starts to get overwhelmed he walks away not saying anything else. For two more months Jimmy remains quiet from everyone else and in no contact with Mary. But during this time he obsesses about her more and more thinking about her every five minutes on each day. At the beginning of the third month he decides to finally pursue her. He writes her a poem and brings it to the school. His plan is to see her in the café and read it to her. That day when he sees her sitting in the cafeteria he sits next to her and pulls out the poem he wrote and reads it. He reads "You're the most beautiful girl anyone could find, which is no dispute, oh my god you are so cute, you have the most beautiful smile as can be, those dimples I love to see, you may be wondering how can this be but it's you as the thriller, you Mary Miller". All of Mary's friends stand up pointing and laughing at Jimmy. Mary sits in silence once again unsure on what to say. Out of embarrassment Jimmy gets up and storms out of the cafeteria. The next day he plans to try it again. Then in the morning when he sees her in the hallway he sees her holding hands with the quarterback of the school football team named Craig. He walks be them quickly to pass by. From this and the embarrassment of the other day Jimmy becomes more isolated and anti social from everyone. As a result he never talks to Mary face to face anymore but watches her in a growing relationship with Craig as they become close. During this Jimmy's obsession for her grows more and more. Each year of high school that goes by he never talks to her but instead watches on other people in her life besides boyfriends. Then on the day of graduation as seniors when it's time to meet up with families after the ceremony Jimmy stares on at Mary's family as they hug and congratulate her. On this day after graduation Jimmy follows Mary and her family all the way to there house in a car that he had stolen. He parks down the street watching on as they all go into the house. In the glove compartment he pulls out a revolver. He gets out the car discretely walking up to the front door of the house. He stands there from a minute. Then he finally kicks the door open. Mary's father goes up to the door to see who it is. Jimmy fires three shots into his chest. Mary and her younger brother both run into her bedroom and lock the door. In the kitchen Mary's mother hides under the counter. Jimmy runs up to her and shoots her in the back of the head. She dies instantly as Mary's father slowly starts to bleed to death. Jimmy runs up to Mary's bedroom door and breaks through it. He aims the revolver at both Mary and her younger brother. He snatches her brother by the wrist and pushes him out of the bedroom. He then grabs Mary by the throat and pushes her down on the bed pressing the revolver up against her forehead. He rips off her shirt and unbuttons her pants. Jimmy awakens out of this moment now realizing this is all a day dream. He is still sitting in the car with all this going through his mind. He puts the revolver back in the glove compartment. As he slowly starts to cry he thinks of what it would be like to be with Mary and to be accepted by her family. He then drives away pass the house as Mary her family continue to celebrate. Jimmy gets out of the car in the middle of the street and throws the revolver away in a trash barrel. The next year Jimmy gets enrolled into college and makes effort to be closer to his parents and as far as dating goes he decides to stay committed to family first and then only wants to meet someone only of his life is together again.

The End


Tired of Dreaming


"My name is James Monroe and I'm an artist". "I grew up in a small town or I should say small towns that I can't remember". "I never had much but only a paint brush and any color I found use for". "My life long dream is to move to California and open up my own art gallery". "One thing I remember is my grandmother telling me as long as I graduate from school and always make honest choices then I can do anything". "Unfortunately like most of my family members I didn't have my grandmother for much long". "At age seventeen I dropped out of high school and had attempted to pursue my art career full time". "But at that time I only got offers from a freelance agency who promised me as long as I came out with a certain amount of money to give them then they'll promote the first few paintings I've finished but after I saved up the money to give them I never heard from them since and none of my paintings were sold". "During the next ten years from motel to rest stop and car ride to long hikes I've been working odd jobs and saving up each year so I can finally move to California". "Reaching closer to the eleventh year I finally was able to save up fifty six hundred dollars so that I can buy a bus ticket and maybe even rent an apartment". "When I get down there my plan is to start out opening a stand on the beach displaying my newest paintings". James purchases a bus ticket at the station to the first bus going to Los Angeles. When he gets there he gets off a stop that's at the beach. He gets off the bus carrying one bag of clothes and rolling a luggage with his paintings in it. He looks around at the beach seeing all the different types of people and events that are going on. After he leaves the beach he walks around looking at apartments that have "For Rent" signs on them. He sees one that has an upstairs balcony. He writes down the phone number listed on the sign. For the next two days he goes through the process of paper work and making a payment of a security deposit and moving furniture in. In the living room he hangs up all of his paintings. Later that night he works on a new painting symbolizing his new arrival to Los Angeles which is a fictionalized setting of the beach. He paints a red sky with blacks clouds that hover over the water of the beach. He also paints the background scenery in dark with black paint on one side and the other side he paints with light colors like gold on the same side as a figure of a man representing him. In the painting as the figure of the man walks closer to the dark side the waves of the ocean rises up and turn into a brighter blue color. The other paintings he plans to display is of a long road with a variety of different people walking together similar to the roads he hitchhiked on. The two other paintings he has are of fantasy designed backgrounds of a forest fire and a snow covered mountain that has an illusion of a man's face. The next day he opens up his stand on the beach with his paintings held up by easels. He waits hour after hour waiting for a customer. By the mid afternoon A surfer carrying his surf board walks up to the stand looking at the painting of the forest fire. "I like this one". "If you're interested it's on sale for one hundred fifty bucks". The surfer laughs. "Dude, nobody out here is going to buy any of this no matter how good these are". "Yeah and why's that"? "Most of the people around here don't really have the appreciation for art and culture". "Well that's too bad cause I worked ten years to get here so I can just try to make a living off of this". "If you really need to make some money I know where you can go". "Where's that? "I know a few people around and they could always use some extra help". "Okay well I'm welling to do what I got to". "What's your name dude"? "I'm James". "My name is Danny". They shake hands. "Maybe now I can show you around to some new friends". "Sure I just have to bring these back to my apartment, it's close by here". "Alright let's do it"! James packs up the paintings and brings them back to the apartment while Danny follows him. James puts the paintings back into the luggage and locks the door on his way out. "So Danny, where are we going"? "To a friend that lives a couple blocks from here". A few minutes later they both walk up to this party at Villa playing loud music. They come in through the back yard where people are swimming in a pool. As they walk by everyone James looks at every girl in a bikini. They walk inside upstairs to a bedroom. Danny calls out the name "Stevie, Stevie"! A man comes out of a large closet in the bedroom. "Whose your friend Danny"? "This is James I just met him today". Stevie shakes hands with James. "I was stopping by because I heard you needed a new delivery boy". James taps Danny on the shoulder. "Delivering what exactly"? Stevie picks up a package held inside a satchel and hands it to James. "This is a package that you deliver to each specified location listed on an address book in there". "Do you mind me asking what this is"? Stevie opens the top part of the satchel revealing the package to be bagged pounds of marijuana. "Only agree if you can handle it but now it's either a yes or a no". "No problem I can handle this, it's just some grass I guess". Stevie and Danny both look at each other and laugh. Danny and James both go back downstairs and outside. "So when do I start"? "Right now as a matter of fact". Danny points to a bicycle chained to the gate. "Are you good with bikes"? "Yeah I've used them before". Danny unchains the bicycle off the gate and wheels it up to James. "Remember the address book is inside the bag and let me know when your done I'll just be here". James takes the address book out of the satchel and reads the first one. He gets on the bicycle and rides to it. For each delivery he either knocks on a door to an apartment or meets someone at their car dividing each amount they ask for. By the time James finishes all of the deliveries he counts all of the cash he received which a total amount of ten thousand dollars. Then he rides all the way back to Stevie's villa. Danny sees him from the backyard and walks up the front to approach him. "So how did you do"? "I got it all right here". He hands Danny all of the cash. Danny smiles with excitement. "Excellent job man come back inside". They go back inside upstairs to Stevie's room. Danny places the cash on a side table in the room. "Stevie I think I picked a keeper he made it through each delivery". "Hey well not bad for the first time". Stevie picks up the cash and counts it and hands James a half of it. "This is for you and we'll keep in touch for next time". "Thanks guys". Danny and James go outside to the pool. "You know James for your good work I want to reward with something else". Danny points to one of the bikini girls by the pool. "Her name is Beth and I would like you to meet her". "Okay sure". They both walk up to her. "Beth this is our new friend James". Beth shakes hands with

James. "We were just wondering if you wanted to keep him some company tonight". James turns head quickly towards Danny. Beth laughs. "I'm not too busy tonight where do you live James"? "My apartment is just a couple blocks away from here". "It's a date then". Later that night Beth and James sit in the living room of the apartment drinking wine. "My life long goal was to always move out here and start my own art gallery". "That's sounds cool everyone else I know just wants to party or get wasted". "I have it all with me if you wanted to look at some". "Sure I'll check some if it out". James takes the paintings out of the luggage. "This is my newest one". He hands her the painting of the beach. "Wow I like this one". "I did it just the other day". James look at his back porch seeing how bright the moon is. "It looks nice out do you want go out to the porch". They go out through the back porch and sit together on a porch swing. James looks up at moon and stars. "For years I always told everybody I was going to become the next best artist of the century but always got a laughed at afterwards". Beth pours herself another glass of wine. "Sometimes I wish I had better support than I did growing up". "I even ask people sometimes if they ever get tired of dreaming and just really hope that whatever they want to do can just happen with no problems or lies". Beth puts down the glass of wine and moves in closer towards James. He looks at her and they kiss. The next morning James wakes up with Beth laying right beside him. His cell phone rings on the night stand. He picks it up and answers it. "Hello"? On the other line Danny walks on the beach with his cell phone. "Hey James it's me this afternoon stop by and meet my at Stevie's we have another job for you to do". "Alright I'll see you then". They both hang up. James looks over at Beth still sleeping and walks into the living room and cleans up moving all of the paintings aside. After he is done cleaning he frames all of the paintings and writes a date on each of them. He also counts what is left over of his money on the kitchen table. He hears Beth waking up. He goes into the bedroom. "Good morning babe". "Hey good morning". "You left your purse in the living room I put it on the table". "Actually I have to go soon". "Yeah I have to get ready for this afternoon anyway". They both walk back into the living room. Beth sees the cash on the kitchen table. She walks over to grab her purse. "I'll walk you out I just have to use the bathroom". James goes into the bathroom. Beth quickly puts the cash into her purse dropping one of the hundred dollar bills on the floor. She closes her purse and stands by the door. James comes out of the bathroom. "It's getting late I better hurry". "Okay let me walk you out". They both go outside. "Hey, before you go I think you forgot something to give me". Beth nervously stops walking. James walks up to her. He puts his hands on her shoulder. He kisses her on the lips. "I'll see you later". "Bye James". Beth walks away as James watches her leave. Then he goes back in the apartment. He takes off of the framed paintings out of the kitchen and puts them in the closet in his bedroom. He walks back into the kitchen and opens the refrigerator to see what's in it. He looks over and just notices the cash is gone. He sees the hundred dollar bill on the floor and picks it up. He kneels down on the floor and looks under the table but doesn't find anymore. He gets up and punches the wall. He picks up his cell phone and calls  Beth's contact number a few times but never gets an answer. Later in the afternoon he goes over Stevie's and meets Danny in the backyard near the pool. "Hey have you seen that girl Beth around"? "No, I thought she was with you". "She was but when she left I think she could've took the money you gave me yesterday". "Come inside we have to talk to Stevie". They go inside and sit on the couch in the living room. Stevie comes in putting a cigarette out in an ash tray on the coffee table. "Stevie we got some bad news; James says he thinks that girl Beth stole the money we gave him yesterday"? "Why is that my problem"? James stands up. "I just want to know if you can find her"! "Come on sit down James". James sits back down. Danny looks at him. "I'm sorry that it happened James but the job we have for you today is worth a lot more than what you did yesterday". "Okay, so what is it"? "There's this doctor we work with and he experiments with our product and today he's going to need more samples but what we need you to do is meet him with a package of fifty pounds and after he pays you we'll split thirty percent of the money with you". Stevie throws a set of keys on James' lap. "You're scheduled to meet him in a half hour so you better get going". "Follow me I'll show you the car you'll be taking". They go out front up to a Mercedes Benz. James gets in the driver's seat. Danny puts the package into the trunk and shuts it. James drives downtown up to a coffee shop. He sees a man sitting up front through the window. He looks at the picture that was given to him. The man he sees matches the picture of the doctor that he has. He looks at him for another minute and drives off. He pulls over into an alley. He takes the package out of the trunk and throws it into a dumpster. He walks away abandoning the car saying to himself "What a bunch of scumbags". He walks to the closest bar and drinks there for a few hours. He takes a taxi back to his apartment. When he gets inside everything is scattered and torn apart with glass all over the floor, urine stains on the wall, and ripped holes in the furniture. James runs into he bedroom seeing it also in the same condition. He goes into his closet seeing all the clothes that were thrown out of it. He takes out the luggage with the paintings in it. They were the same as before. James takes a deep breathe out of relieve. James goes into the living room and sits on the floor. He cries slowly with heavy tears. A few months go by and in a struggle to find work James gets an eviction notice to the apartment. To make some fast money James sells his paintings to a local restaurant. On his way out of the restaurant he sees a newspaper and picks it up. The headline reads "Undercover Agent Posing As A Pharmacist Leads To Narcotic Bust". James looks down seeing a picture of the 'doctor' wearing a badge and being awarded. Below that he sees two more pictures of Danny and Stevie's mug shots. Later that Day Danny walks on the beach looking up at the seagulls flying. When he gets home to the apartment he paints a mural on his wall of himself in the clouds with seagulls drifting away from people down below. James studies and receives his G.E.D in the mail. The following year he takes courses for liberal arts.


The end


Dead End


There was a African American man named Darius Johnson he was born December 8, 1963 in

Watts, California. His father is an activist named Fred Johnson who travels to local churches and his

Mother named Betty Johnson is a middle school teacher who teaches in an all-black segregated school. In 1968 Darius is now five years old. One night he and his parents look out the window of their house and see people rioting with buildings in flames and police cars in a melee with the rioters. Betty picks up Darius and clutches him in her arms. Fred runs into his bedroom and grabs clothes out his wardrobe and packs it in brown suit cases. They all flee the house when shortly after they run out the door a brick smashes through the living room window. One month later they move into a suburban neighborhood with green grass and white picket fences. Darius sits on the curb of the sidewalk and looks around at the neighborhood. He gets up and takes his bicycle out of the garage and rides it a few blocks down the street. While he rides he looks around and sees groups of young black males on each side of the street walking together dressed in black leather coats and wearing fedora hats. He becomes fascinated and stops his bike and looks around more at the people in that other part of the neighborhood and sees young black females wearing dresses and carrying school books. He smiles and raises his eye brows. He gets back on his bike and continues to ride down another block down the remaining street. This time he sees Cadillac cars and a Stutz. Then he sees men in fur coats holding canes and making trades with selifan bags for cash money. After the men make their exchange they walk across the street and go into a social club. Darius puts his bike down and peaks through the door of the social club and sees men and women rolling dice at a table and in the corner the same men wearing the fur coats trade revolvers and knives on a small table. Then he sees a man in a two piece suit walk towards the door. Before the man opens the door Darius runs back to his bike and rides back home. When he walks into the house his parents sit beside each other in the living room. "Darius get your bible, it's time to read the Holy Scripture" says Fred. They all sit at the kitchen table while Fred reads out loud the verses from Psalm 23. Betty puts on her reading glasses sitting across from Fred. Darius looks down at the bible and imagines himself on that street where he saw those people and sees himself driving a black Cadillac with that school girl in the dress sitting in the passenger seat next to him. Betty looks up at Darius and sees him zone out. "Darius, pay attention" said Betty. He looks back down at the bible and searches with his finger at where they left off in the reading. That night when Darius goes to sleep he looks out of his window and looks up at a full moon in the sky. 13 Years Later Los, Angeles California.

Darius walks down the street in the South Central neighborhood with two other male teenagers. "I heard you got accepted into UCLA Darius, what's up with that" asked Ray. "My dad helped me get a scholarship" replied Darius. "What are you studying for" asked Tyrone. "I was thinking about being a lawyer or engineer but I'm not trying to be no preacher" says Darius. Tyrone and Ray both laugh. "You know you got too much religion in your family" remarked Ray. "You know that's true" said Tyrone. "Hey Darius we're going to a party tonight and why don't you come too college boy" suggested Ray. "What time" asked Darius. "It doesn't matter what time it just depends on when you show up" says Tyrone. "Alright I'll be there" said Darius. Later on that night at the party the house is crowded from the inside and outside. Tyrone and Darius walk into the front yard through the gate and squeeze by all the crowd of people dancing. "Look at all the girlies" shouted Tyrone. They both make it to the porch of the house and go inside. "Follow me" Tyrone says to Darius. They both walk in the kitchen and each get a red solo cup. Tyrone puts his drink in the air and yells out "Stop the music, I'd like to propose a toast my boy Darius, he's going to college"! Everybody at the party cheers for him and they all raise their cups up for him. "Thanks man" said Darius under his breathe. Ray comes in the kitchen and looks

at Darius. "Come on now Darius this is your night, you need to talk to one of these females" says Ray. Darius smiles and takes a sip of his drink. "Let's get back to the party" said Tyrone. The music plays louder and everybody goes back to dancing. Darius walks around sipping his drink more and more until he sees this girl outside leaned up against the gate talking with two other girls. He walks outside and approaches her. "Hey ladies" says Darius. They all look at him and wave their hands. He looks at the girl he saw from the inside. "What's your name" asked Darius. "Tracy" replied the girl. The two other girls walk away and join the other people dancing in the yard. "And your name is" asked Tracy. "I'm Darius" he replied. "Are you the one going to UCLA" asked Tracy. "Yeah, so you heard about" asked Darius. "That's what everybody's been talking about" says Tracy. "I guess so" said Darius sarcastically. "Are you excited about it" asked Tracy. "I kind of am, are you enjoying yourself tonight" asked Darius. "Yeah, it's about time we had a decent party for some type of good cause" replied Tracy. "You doing anything after the party" asked Darius. After the party Darius and Tracy sneak into the window of his bedroom. He picks her up by the waist and helps her climb through the window. After she gets in he jumps through it head first. Then he gets up off the floor and turns the lights on. Tracy walks up to him and kisses him on the lips. He responds by kissing her back and then they both lock their lips tightly and continue to repeat it over and over. Darius moves his head lower and starts to kiss her on the neck. Then he picks her up and lays her down on his bed and takes his shirt off. The next day he wakes up and looks on the other side of his bed and sees nothing but wrinkled sheets and his window wide open. He sits up and gets out of bed and puts a bath robe on. One month later in the afternoon he sits at the kitchen table of the house and studies out of a S.A.T. book. In the kitchen the telephone rings and Betty walks up to it and answers. "Hello" asked Betty. "Is Darius there" asked the caller. "Yes, who's this" asked Betty. "It's Tyrone" revealed the caller. "Hold on a minute" says Betty. She looks at Darius. "Your friend Tyrone wants to talk to you" she said. Darius closes the book and puts his pen down and gets up. Betty hands him the phone and walks out of the kitchen. "Hey Tyrone" says Darius. Tyrone sits beside his bed on the phone in his room. "I don't know if you know yet but after you left the party with that girl Ray left too but nobody seen him afterwards, have you" asked Tyrone. Darius scratches his head. "No I haven't, I wonder what he was doing" says Darius. "I don't know but I'm just calling everybody to check if they seen him lately" said Tyrone. "That's why I keep telling everybody that we all need to stop playing around and act like we have some sense once in a while" replied Darius. "Look man I know all that but for now we got to think about Ray" says Tyrone. "Well I just want to let you guys know that I don't like where you guys hang out sometimes because it doesn't you cool and stupid stuff like this happens" complained Darius. "Look man you don't have to act like my daddy I was just asking if seen Ray around" replied Tyrone. "Why do you think I left early with that girl last night in the first place" asked Darius angrily. He hangs up the phone and sits back down at the table and opens the book back up. Fred and Betty both come in the kitchen and approach Darius. "Son your mother and I are going to another speech engagement" says Fred. "Okay pop" replied Darius. They both walk out of the kitchen and leave the house. Darius flips back to the page where he left off and continues to write with his pen. Fred and Betty both walk inside a community center downtown. Betty sits in the front row in front of a podium. Fred stands behind the podium and watches as more and more people come in and form an audience in the room. Then he picks a microphone and switches it on. "The reason we are gathered here tonight are two reasons" announced Fred. Two more people walk in and join the audience. One is a police officer and the other is a minister wearing a clerical collar. "First I would like to thank the entire guest and supporters who've shared their time to be with us tonight and what I want to talk about first tonight is the way of overcoming" says Fred. Betty looks up at him and nods her head in agreement. "My wife and I who is sitting up front are not originally from here but we've seen the potential of madness that can happen and how I know this is because me, my wife, and son seen a race riot right in front of our door step and like many other moments in this part of history it drove us and many others out of their homes" explained Fred. "I'm not saying that where me nor my wife is from was any better but that night spoke to me and made a change as I was packing clothes out of my own wardrobe and rushing to protect my own family and those two reasons are potential self-justice and senseless anarchy that's not just political but within each and every one of us" described Fred. One of the spectators up front raises their hand. "Yes" asks Fred. "Did you and your family get hurt from the incident" asked the spectator. "If we didn't move the way we did then we would of" answered Fred. Back at the house there's a knock on the door. Darius gets up once again and answers the door. Tracy stands there on the door step with a tear in her left eye. "What's a matter Tracy" asked Darius. She sniffles and rubs her eyes. "Can I come in" asked Tracy. "Yeah come in" said Darius. He moves aside and lets her in. They both sit on the couch in the living room. "What happened" asked Darius. She looks up at him. "I'm pregnant" says Tracy. Darius' face freezes in silence and slightly twitches.


24 Years Later FBI Head Quarters Los Angeles, CA


One of the agents walks into an office and knocks on the side of the door. "Hey Danny, I got a new assignment for you" says the agent. He puts the files and a folder on Danny's desk and leaves his office. Danny opens the folder and goes through the files and sees a poster template of a wanted man named Juan Hernandez. In the shooting range of the bureau Danny wears a FBI cap and puts on ear muffs. He pulls out his Glock 22 out of his holster and begins to fire at the cardboard dummy moving towards him. He scores by hitting the head and torso of the target and reloads the clip back in and aims shoots faster at the next target. The next day Danny gathers around with the other agents and they all equip themselves with bullet proof vests and arm themselves with 12 gauge shotguns and put their hand guns in their holsters. Then they all go into the garage and get into their GMC Yukon and drive off. They drive through the sections of the South Central neighborhood and pull over in front of this house. One of the agents in the car looks at the poster template of Juan Hernandez and looks at the address of the house. "This should be it" says the agent. They all get out and form a line and strategically walk through the gate of the front yard. Three agents including Danny walk up to the house and to the door. Two of the agents stand by on each left and right side. Danny stands in front of the door pointing his shotgun. The other agents are kneeled down in the yard. Danny knocks on the door twice. While he knocks he has an image in his head of what the suspect did which is shooting a gang member in the face in an alley and runs in the middle of the street away from a police squad car and gets pinned down by a single police officer. The officer gets out of the squad car and aims his firearm at Juan and yells "Put your weapon down and get on the ground"! Juan throws his pistol on the sidewalk and puts his hands on his head and drops down to his knees. The officer puts his gun away and walks up to him and takes out a pair of hand cuffs. Right before the officer locks one of his wrist Juan pulls out a switch blade knife from his back pocket and stabs the officer in the right leg. The officer falls to the ground and reaches for his gun. Juan turns around and drives the knife into the officer's lower stomach. The officer screams in pain. Then Juan gets up and picks up his gun on the sidewalk and stuffs it between the front of his pants and his shirt. He hears sirens in the background and runs across the street into one of the residence's yard and jumps over the fence. Other Police officers arrive on the scene and see the police officer on the ground bleeding profusely from his leg and stomach. Juan continues to run and spots a family on their porch and takes his gun out and points it at them. He shushes them and orders all of them to go back in the house. They do as he says and they all go into the house. He has them all sit down on the couch. Then he looks out the window. Danny kicks the door open and runs inside the house. The two other agents come in and guard his back. A woman and a little girl are sitting on the couch watching TV. They both look at Danny and the agents. Danny puts his finger over his lips and shushes them. The two other agents escort the woman and little outside and the rest of the agents come inside the house. Danny looks around the house and sees a staircase on the right side of the living room. He approaches it slowly and everybody else lines up behind him and follows his lead up the stairs. Upstairs there's one bedroom with the door closed. Behind that door Juan aims a 9mm pistol at the door as he hears footsteps coming closer and closer. Danny signals with his fist making a gesture to halt. Everybody stops and Danny points his 12 gauge at the door. Juan pulls the trigger and fires three shots through the door. Danny jerks his body back and screams "Look out"! He aims his 12 gauge back at the door and fires a shot at the door. The bullet hole appears larger than the bullet holes from Juan's 9mm. Juan reacts and slips on the floor and falls. He gets up quickly and opens the window of the bedroom and jumps out into the alley outside. Danny kicks the door open and runs into the room. The agents run in there behind him. "He went out the window" yelled Danny. Juan runs into the alley and turns around. He shoots his gun towards the window. Danny jumps back and shoots another shell out the window. Then he puts his left leg over the window and jumps out. Juan turns back around and runs in the opposite direction. Danny chases after him and tries to get a clean shot of him while he runs. Juan runs into the street and nearly gets hit by a passing car. Danny stops running and avoids getting hit by another car. Juan runs into the next alley across and sees three LAPD officers up ahead on foot running towards him. The street clears and Danny runs across the street towards the alley. Juan turns around and sees Danny coming closer and the police officers moving in. He presses his gun against his head and pulls the trigger. Blood splatters and his lifeless body drops to the ground and he lies there in a pool of blood. Danny and the police officers circle around him. Danny looks down and stares at Juan's fresh corpse. Five minutes later the ambulance and more police officers arrive on the scene and put Juan in a body bag and strap him onto a stretcher and wheel him into an ambulance truck. Danny and all the other FBI agents stand by their vehicle. Danny leans up against the hood of the truck and looks down. One of the other agents walks by him and stops and looks at him and asks "Are you okay"? Danny nods his head yes. He turns his head and looks behind him and sees all the other agents getting into the truck. He sits up and wipes sweat off his forehead and walks around the truck and gets into the back seat of the truck. Later on in the evening of that day Danny drives his casual car which is a black dodge intrepid into a suburban neighborhood and parks it behind a black Range Rover in a drive way. He gets out of the car and holds his black blazer in between his hand and fore arm. He walks onto the steps of the porch and goes into the house. "Rochelle, where you at girl" asked Danny. "I'm in the kitchen and dinner is on the table" replied Rochelle. He walks into the kitchen and sees her set two plates on the table. She puts forks next to the plates and walks up to Danny. "Hi baby" says Danny. They both kiss on the lips. "I'll be right back, I'm going get changed real quick" said Danny. He walks upstairs and goes into their bedroom and takes off his tie and throws his blazer on the bed. Then he sits on the bed and takes off his shoes. In front of him is their bed with a mirror hanging on the wall with a picture of his adoptive parents taped to the mirror. He looks up at it and smiles. He gets up off the bed and walks back downstairs and goes into the kitchen and sees a bowl of steaming macaroni and cheese and a platter with a pile of grilled salmon, and another steaming bowl of green beans. Rochelle sits at the head of the table and pours herself a glass of white wine. Danny sits on the left side of the table next to her and reaches for the platter of grilled salmon and puts each one of them on her plate and his plate. Then he picks up a large spoon on the table and scoops the macaroni and cheese on their plates and then scoops the green beans on both their plates. "How was work today" asked Rochelle. "It was okay but one of the suspects committed suicide today" replied Danny. Rochelle squints her face. "Really, I'm sorry about that baby" said Rochelle. "Yeah I know, but it wasn't like he had any better chances but I didn't expect him to take his life in front of everybody like that" says Danny. "People saw it" asked Rochelle. "It was in broad daylight and I think he had a girlfriend and children downstairs in the house or better yet it could have been his own wife" explained Danny. "That's horrible" said Rochelle. Danny cuts his salmon in pieces and takes his first bite. Rochelle gathers her macaroni and begins eating as well. "It's like he did what he did and in the end he will have a consequence but other people who care about him shouldn't have to" says Danny. "I'm sorry to hear that" said Rochelle. "But it's also by job to protect people who get hurt from people like that" says Danny strictly. "As long as you come home safe to me every night then I'm happy" replied Rochelle. Danny lays his left hand on the table and she lifts her arm up on the table and holds it with her left hand. "Next week my niece and nephew Janet and Roger are coming over and they want to know if you'll have the pool set up for them by then" informed Rochelle. "Yeah I can do that for them" says Danny. 24 years ago back to that day when Darius walks on the campus of UCLA he goes into an orientation class of law and justice. He sits in the third row up front of the classroom and they watch a video formatted into a projector on the wall of court reenactments and how lawyers presented themselves to clients while in the court room.

Los Angeles Superior Courthouse Present Day

A middle aged Darius sits beside his client which is the defendant. On the other table the female plaintiff cries and wipes her with tissues. It's now the plaintiff's lawyer's turn to talk. He stands up and faces Judge Jefferson. "Your honour it's clearly evident that the defendant has a criminal record which states what he's capable of" says the lawyer of the plaintiff. "It doesn't matter what the defendant is capable of counselor or what he knows for but it matters on if you have any proof or not" replied Judge Jefferson. Darius stands up. "Your honour let me state that my client is well insured from the passing of his mother and may we consider that the plaintiff could be using this as a scam for their own benefit" blurted out Darius. "Objection, what does that have to do with anything" asked the lawyer of the plaintiff. "What it has to do with is the fact that if she wins this case then my client will be fined which would make her financial stable" explained Darius. The jury talks loudly and so do the viewers. The judge slams down his gavel and yells "Order"! Darius stands back up and looks back up at the judge."Bottom line your honour there is no physical evidence that my client was with the plaintiff that night nor any physical evidence of contact" says Darius. He opens the folder on the table and pulls out two pieces of paper. "What I have here your honour is a police report and restraining order that states our own evidence that the plaintiff has been harassing my client" said Darius. The bailiff walks up to Darius and takes the two pieces of paper and hands them to the judge. Judge Jefferson looks at both of them and reads through. The plaintiff now cries heavily. The judge hands the papers back to the bailiff. "Well Counselor Johnson and Mr. Andrews I have no choice but to dismiss the case and any pending charges, court is now dismissed" says Judge Jefferson. He picks the gavel up again and slams it down. The plaintiff and her lawyer walk out the room first. Everybody gets up and begins to exit. Darius and his client shake hands. Darius picks his suit case up from the floor and places it on the table and puts his folder and all of his files in his suit case and closes it shut. When gets out of the courthouse the media and reporters follow him outside. "Mr. Johnson what do you have to say about your victory" asked reporter #1. "It feels positively reasonable" answers Darius. "Is your client really guilty" asked reporter #2. "No comment" replied Darius. "If you were to end the case in any other way what would you do" asked reporter #3. "It's too much of a simple case to end it in any other because like they say it is what it is" says Darius. Two people in the crowd of the media take pictures and make flashes. "Now ladies and gentle I really have to get home, no more questions please" told by Darius. He walks away and goes into the parking lot and gets in his car which is a black Nissan Ultima and drives away. He drives into a suburban neighborhood and parks in a drive way. He gets out and carries his suit case and opens the door of the house and walks in. "Anybody still here" asked Darius out loud. "We're down here" answered two younger girls in the basement. He walks to the basement door on the right side of the living room and opens it and walks down the stairs. "What are y'all down doin' down here" asked Darius. "You never took us down here, it's nice" replied one of the girls. "Do you have a ride home" asked Darius. "No" they both answered at the same time. "I'll guy you two a cab" said Darius. They both walk upstairs. "I'll call y'all tomorrow" shouted Darius. "Okay" they shouted back. In the basement Darius sees a black book sticking out the shelf. He walks up to it and takes it out of the shelf and opens it. He flips to the first page of the book and sees a picture of his parents sitting together in church and smiles. The phone rings upstairs in the living room. Darius puts the photo album back in the shelf and walks upstairs to the living room. He picks up the phone and answers it. "Hello" asks Darius. On the other line is his client Mr. Andrews. "Hello Mr. Johnson, can I talk to you for minute" asks Mr. Andrews. "Sure Lucas" replied Darius. "I need a favor from you" says Lucas. "What is it" asks Darius. "First I would like to thank you for getting me off today but I have this friend named Chris who can use your help" explained Lucas. "What did he do" asks Darius. "He got into some trouble in New York; you know weapon possession, assault and battery" replied Lucas. "If that was in New York then what's he doing in L.A." asks Darius. "He took a flight up here to get away from the heat but he knows eventually he might get caught which means he needs a lawyer just in case and his flight lands tomorrow" says Lucas. "Have him meet me the day after tomorrow" ordered Darius. In the lounge room of the bureau Danny sits at the eating table next to a fellow agent. "Hey Dan, what was your first job before this one" asks the agent. "I was a LAPD officer" replied Danny. "What was that like" asks the agent. "It was a regular police job up until this one night when my partner and I did a routine traffic stop" said Danny. "What happened" asked the agent. A LAPD squad car pulls over a red custom made BMW E35 AVM. Danny and his partner get out of the squad car and flash lights into the car they pulled over. Danny walks up to the passenger seat and his partner walks up to the driver's seat and knocks on the window. The driver is an African American male teenager with corn rows. He reaches into the glove compartment and pulls out only his driver's license and hands it to Danny's partner. Danny walks around the car and his partner gives him the driver's license. Danny goes back into the squad car and looks it up on the computer. Then Danny looks up and sees the teenager on his knees with his hands behind his head. Danny's partner sees a piece of black leather through the cracks of the teenager's fingers and grabs him by the hood of his sweat shirt and slams him to the pavement and whips his pistol out of his holster. Danny sees a black leather wallet and a folded piece of paper on the ground next to it. His partner points his pistol at the teenager's head. Danny takes out his pistol and yells out "What are you doing"! His partner looks up at him and aims his pistol him. Danny lowers his pistol and fires one shot into his partner's right leg. The teenager jumps up in a startled reaction while as he falls to the ground. Danny's partner lies on the ground holding his left hand against his right leg. Danny runs up towards the teenager's direction and bends down and picks up the black leather wallet and paper. Danny's partner lifts his head up and aims his pistol at Danny's head. The teenager screams "Watch out"! Danny turns around and fires a shot into his partner's upper torso. His head and arm drop down and blood oozes out of his right leg and chest as he lies there dying. Danny unfolds the piece of paper which turns out to be the registration of the car. Back in the lounge room Danny pulls out a pack of cigarettes. "What happened afterwards" asked the agent. "On the dashboard of the squad car there was a camera that recorded the whole thing and the kid we pulled over testified in court as a witness" explained Danny. "What happened to the kid afterwards" asked the agent. "I let him off with a warning" laughed Danny. "Man, that's crazy" replied the agent. "I didn't want to shoot my own partner but it was either him or a kid who couldn't defend himself" says Danny. "I don't know what I would've done if I was in that situation" commented the agent. "Well sometimes we all get into situations when we look back and say I would of done this or I would of changed what I already did if I could but at the

same during those moments like that we hit a dead end and just react" described Danny. "What happened to you partner after you shot him" asked the agent. "He was rushed to the hospital and bled to death on the way there" replied Danny. "So nothing happened to you" asked the agent. "No, because they looked at it as my doing an act of police brutality and if he would actually have shot the kid it would be another case of racial profiling when the kid had no weapons in the first place and the city of L.A. didn't want to have another one of those on their hands" answered Danny. "Well, if I asked any other agent in the bureau what their former jobs were I would get a security guard, school teacher, or maybe even a job at MacDonald's when they were a kid or something but I think I might like yours the best" says the agent. Danny takes a cigarette out of the pack and puts it in his mouth and pulls out a lighter. Two days later Darius and Lucas are standing in the lobby of the airport and look at the passengers exiting the plane. As all the passengers enter inside the building they look around for Chris in the line of passengers. In front of the line is a light skinned black man wearing a black leather coat. Lucas points at him. "That's him, hey Chris" yelled out Lucas. Chris walks up to them. "This is the man I been telling you about" says Lucas. Darius holds out his hand. "I'm district attorney Johnson" greeted Darius. He and Chris shake hands. "Let's go to my place" says Lucas. Darius, Lucas, and Chris sit in a small apartment with clothes all over the floor and empty beer bottles. Lucas and Chris sit next to each other on the couch and Darius sits across from them on a sofa. "Now I know what you said about assault and possession but if you want me to represent you then you have to tell me the full story" says Darius. "I was walking down the street in Queens and I go into this corner store" replied Chris. He visualizes it as he tells it. In that corner store he kicks the door open and pulls out a silver Colt pistol and draws it at the store clerk. He jumps over the counter and grabs the clerk by the collar and points into the clerk's direction a button under the counter. The clerk reaches under the counter and pushes the button. Behind the clerk's foot a piece of the floor board opens up and a set of stairs going downward appears. Chris bashes the clerk in the back of the head with his pistol and walks down the stairs. When he makes it to the bottom of the stairs he sees two men sitting at a table with a pile of scattered cash and a revolver on the right side of the table. Chris aims his gun at them. They both look at him and the man sitting on the right side of the table reaches for the revolver. Chris immediately shoots in the chest and stomach. The man falls back in his chair down to the floor. The other man gets up and runs. Chris shoots him in the back and walks up to him and shoots him in the back of the neck. Blood splatters on the cash. Chris turns around and grabs dollar bills off the table and stuffs it in his pocket. NYPD squad cars pull up outside with their sirens flashing. Chris looks around for and exit and sees a door with a chain and lock around it. Chris shoots the chain and lock and kicks the door open. He runs out the door into an alley with a dumpster and tucks the gun into the back of his pants. The memory fades out. "So you mean murder and robbery instead of assault and possession" asked Darius. "From what Chris and I discussed we came up with a story that you can tell the court" says Lucas. "Which is" asked Darius. Chris leans forward. "I went into that store as a vigilante to stop those pushers and I shot them in self-defense because they pulled a gun out on me first" explained Chris. "What about when you held up that clerk, isn't that just armed robbery within itself" asked Darius. "If we mention that clerk was in on it with that kind of thing going on in his store then he's guilty too" replied Chris. "I'll try but there's no guarantee the jury is going to buy that" recommended Darius. "Then you'll have to make them" says Chris. He reaches into his pocket and tosses a bank roll of cash onto Darius' lap with a rubber band wrapped around it. Danny sits in his office on his computer looking at captured suspects. Darius lies in his bed while a woman sits on the other side of the bed putting high heels on her feet. "You getting ready to leave" asked Darius. "Yeah" replied the woman. "I have this new client from New York and I have to convince the jury that it was self-defense from him taking the law into his own hands" complained Darius. The woman counts a fifty dollar bill followed up with twenty dollar bills in her hands and gets up. "I might not like the guy but it's a favor for a friend" says Darius. The woman walks towards the door she sighs and whispers "good night Darius" under her breathe. Back in Danny's office he updates the profile photo of Juan Hernandez as deceased. Then he

logs out into a blank computer screen and opens the drawer of the desk and takes out a 9mm pistol and loads in the clip and puts it in his holster. Back in Darius' room he leans towards the night stand and grabs a cigar. Right before he puts it in his mouth he sees the woman's purse on the floor and giggles. She comes back in the room and picks it up. "I guess I should be thankful because it pays my bills including you" commented Darius. She straps her purse around her shoulder and throws up her middle finger at Darius and leaves the room again. Darius gets out of the bed and lights his cigar and smokes it while he walks up to the front window of the bedroom. He looks outside of it and sees her getting into the back seat of a taxi cab. In Danny's office he gets up and pushes his chair into his desk and looks out of the window at a scaffolding and the metropolis of the city. Chris and Lucas sit at a bar counter next to each other. "I'm telling you man, he's good and he'll help you through this" suggested Lucas. "When he won your case what was it about" asked Chris. "My ex-girlfriend kept harassing me and she would lie and tell people I would abuse her and that I'm associated with a bunch of criminals" replied Lucas. "Is all that true" asked Chris. "I wouldn't abuse her but I have to say that I got my hands dirty a few times but it's not like I could afford a lawyer like Darius with a normal job anyway" admitted Lucas. "I know how that is" mumbled Chris. "Do you regret what you do back in Queens" asked Lucas. "Well besides me just needing the money I had beef with that whole crew because they snitched on one of my friends to keep the cops off their back and who's to say if I was next" explained Chris. The bartender gives them each a full shot glass. "Here's to our friend attorney Johnson" says Lucas. They both hold their glasses up and make a toast. Santa Monica, California At a jewelry store Lucas and his girlfriend walk in the front entrance and look around at all the merchandise. Lucas whispers into her ear "This place will do". They separate and she walks up to store counter and asks the employee "Are you guys hiring"? Lucas walks around the store and scopes out all the jewelry. Later on in the evening of that day two men wearing black ski masks walk around the same jewelry store that is closed. They pick the lock of the back door and break in. When they get inside, they run through the storage room and go into the front floor of the store. The alarm sounds off and they both turn flashlights on and smash open the glass of the showcase displays and snatch chains and necklaces quickly into a duffel bag. Then they run out the same way they came back in and bump into one of the boxes on the storage shelves and knock it down. The box breaks open and a few cullinan diamonds fall out of it. They both turn around and put them in the duffel bag. In addition, run out the back door. When they get outside a black Ford truck pulls up and they get in the backseat and drive off. Lucas' girlfriend is the driver. Both robbers take their masks off and the one sitting on the left in the backseat is Lucas who is also carrying the duffel bag. "Good job baby" Lucas says to her. "How should we split this" asks Lucas' partner. Lucas looks at him, opens his side of the door, and shoves him out the car. He rolls in the middle of the street and the following cars in traffic nearly run him over. Lucas and his girlfriend both laugh. The next day Lucas and his girlfriend sit on a motel bed next to the duffel bag. "The best part is when you pushed him out the truck, but really how did you want to split this between us" she asks him. Lucas stands up off the bed and grabs the duffel bag. "Baby look, you could have showed up a little earlier with the truck" he says. "What do you mean" she asks. "You didn't do a horrible job or anything but it was a risk of me getting busted" he replies. He walks out the door with the duffel bag. The bartender serves Chris another drink. "Ever since then she won't let it go and she started all this" says Lucas.

The End